LIFE'S LITERACY LESSONS

Stories and Poems for Teachers

STEVEN L. LAYNE

STENHOUSE PUBLISHERS
PORTLAND, MAINE

Stenhouse Publishers
www.stenhouse.com

Library of Congress Cataloging-in-Publication Data

Layne, Steven L.
  Life's literacy lessons : stories and poems for teachers / Steven L. Layne. -- [First
Stenhouse Publishers edition].
     pages cm
  ISBN 978-1-57110-988-0 (hard cover : alk. paper) -- ISBN 978-1-57110-989-7
(e-book) 1. Literacy programs--Poetry. 2. Teaching. 3. Teachers. I. Title.
  PS3612.A96L55 2013
  811'.54--dc23
                              2013000878

Book design by Blue Design, Portland, Maine (www.bluedes.com)

Manufactured in the United States of America

19 18 17 16 15 14 13   9 8 7 6 5 4 3 2 1

For Judson University's MLIT students and graduates,
who always leave me inspired, and for the MLIT faculty,
without whom the dream could never have taken flight.

CONTENTS

A WORD FROM STEVEN

T his is the most interesting book I have ever developed. It began, really, with a poem I wrote in 1994 called "Read to Them." That poem appeared in *The Reading Teacher,* and a lot of permissions were granted over the years to use it for a variety of purposes. Those permission requests sent a message to me that people in our field appreciated the power a poem has to bring a dynamic message forward. And so, in 2001 the original edition of this book was released by the International Reading Association. It became one of their best-selling titles—given to new and veteran literacy teachers and leaders to inspire them, used by some of the nation's leading literacy voices to launch their professional workshops, and heralded by many university professors for providing the opening to some of their favorite lectures. Time needles at books like everything else, though, and what once was new becomes older and receives less attention. In 2010, the book was put out of print—a sad reality of the publishing industry that all authors must face.

Well, here we are in 2013, and readers can hold the book in their hands again thanks to what I'll refer to as the "resurrection power" of Stenhouse and my editor, Bill Varner, who hears the word "no" about as well as I do. This is twice he has made me a believer; next time I will just listen to him from the start. If you're holding this book for the first time, it's all new to you—YEAH, YOU! If you are familiar with the original version, you should be wondering (at least I would be), "What's changed? Did they take out my favorite piece? Did they just stamp a new copyright and cover on this book and rerelease it?"

Here are the answers to those burning questions. Everyone's favorites are still included; it was a conscious decision on our part to include all of the original material—how else could we be sure we were not removing *your* favorite piece? What's new? Each of the five sections in the book has new lead material. Not only are there new poems, appropriate to the literacy issues of our day, but there are also longer pieces of prose—anecdotes—written in the voice and style that is typical of the stories shared in many of my keynote addresses. So, let's add this up: six new "trendy" literacy poems + five new anecdotes + all of the original material. I hope you'll keep a copy at your favorite place to write, another in your classroom, and a third in one of the many bags you're always lugging around, to read when you have a spare minute or—better yet—to give to someone who needs it. When is the perfect time for a literacy lesson? End of the year, beginning of the year, holidays, birthdays, workshops, conferences, seminars, graduation, retirement . . . or any time you just need a little lift, I'd say.

In the words of my favorite superintendent, "Teach the children and treat them well."

ABOUT BEGINNING AND EARLY READING

Miss Porter . . . and Miss Hickory

She had a green frayed rug, as I remember it, and a rocking chair. Her hair was light brown and curled close up on her head in what the ladies of the day called a "permanent." She was a tiny woman, small in stature—but to her first-grade students she had amazing presence. It seemed to me, as I prepared to enter the halls of Willson Elementary school for another year, that one of the universe's most sacred truths was headed my way, and it was this: nobody messes with Mary Lou Porter. My father actually verbalized it for me—and he knew it from personal experience. She had been his teacher, too.

Miss Porter never married in the traditional let's-you-and-I-be-together-forever sense; however, she did have a solemn and committed relationship with the teaching profession. She was married to the job, and she took it very seriously. I didn't much care for her at first. Even as a first grader, I was quite perceptive. I quickly labeled her the no-nonsense, fun-destroying type. I have a vivid memory of being refused bathroom access when I requested it while she was teaching. "There are no restroom privileges during instruction, Steven!" She and I were destined to tangle, and—for much of the first quarter of the school year—we did. I was terribly strong-willed, but so was she, and she was more practiced at successfully exercising her will than I seemed to be. Still, my efforts against the opposition were valiant—they earned me the grade of "D" in reading on my first quarter report from her. The message she scrawled to my parents in the handwritten comment section would translate in today's jargon to "Steven needs to step it up." My mother, being very good friends with what she called a switch and I called a limb from one of the larger trees in our neighborhood, persuaded me that I would indeed step it up. Miss Porter had now solidified herself as my adversary, and

I was determined to make her pay for both the "D" and the comment.

My sweet revenge enacted itself in the form of an SRA Reading Lab that she unveiled in the second quarter of grade one. Vanna White never saw such a modeling job as Miss Porter did with these kits of multicolored cards with stories and questions to answer. Though she did not highlight it for the class, she did mention (those of us poised for vengeance took careful note) that as one advanced in skill level, the card color would change—with completion of *aqua* serving as the mountaintop experience. I strolled past the aqua box, picked up the final card in it, studied the card carefully, and salivated. I would be there before long. I was determined to be the first in our class to make it to-and-through the aqua box. We'd just see what Miss Porter had to say about that little newsflash! Well, I achieved the goal, and she had plenty to say—all very positive. In that crafty teacher way, Miss Porter had apparently been cheering me on throughout what I had thought to be a rather clandestine plan. Somewhere along the way, the adversary became an ally; I hadn't realized teachers were so cagey. I later learned she herself had been an aqua, and this explained a great deal.

Miss Porter read to us each day from her rocking chair. I sat obediently on the green frayed rug and listened but remained a fairly close associate with the fringe. I saw no point in cozying up close to a woman who guarded the bathroom pass with such vigilance. As time passed, and we reached an understanding (aquas stick together), I drew in closer. On the day she began to read aloud from Carolyn Bailey's *Miss Hickory,* I found myself inching through the crowd until I was right at her feet. I remained there throughout the entire book—captivated beyond words by the story of a twig whose head was an acorn. Once I gave her the chance, Miss Porter launched me into a world from which I have never returned—the world of story.

I reached for *Miss Hickory* a few years ago; I'd been thinking of Miss Porter's influence on my life and wanted to reclaim the magic of how it all began. I completed the book, scratching my head in disbelief that this was the story that had so captured me and launched me on my journey toward lifelong reading. It came to me then, in small moments, that the text had been only part of the equation and perhaps not even the most important part. The teacher had been the decisive factor; without Miss Porter, *Miss Hickory* could never again be, for me, all that she had once been. Amazing, isn't it—what a mediocre story and a packaged box of aqua cards can do in the hands of a true magician?

I was with Mary Lou Porter shortly before she died. Confined to bed in a nursing home, she was overjoyed to find her name in the original version of this very book, *Life's Literacy Lessons.* We talked about the magic of *Miss Hickory* and other fond memories of first grade. I hadn't planned on it, but before departing I drew myself up in my chair and queried if she remembered the name of the very first person in my first-grade class to make it all the way to aqua in our SRA reading lab. Ever the charlatan, she pondered for a much longer period of time than I felt was necessary. I burst out that it was ME! Me, me, me, me, me, me, me! *I* was the first to make it to aqua! She reached through the bed rails, patted my hand, gave me an impish grin, and said, "Yes, Steven. Indeed it was you. We aquas stick together."

Yes, we do, Miss Porter. Yes, we do. Even after all these years.

Kindergarten 1.0

Have Circle Time/Morning Meeting
Listen to story about sheep
Chorally read sheep story
Retell sheep story
Listen to Amos McGill tell about his grandfather's sheep farm
Listen to Arliss Pentecost tell about how he played a shepherd in the church play
Listen to Molly Malone tell how she cries when the sheep dies in the *Little Drummer Boy* movie
Listen to Randall Wenkey tell how his dad drinks beer too much
Drink and bathroom break
Snack
Color sheep
Cut out sheep
Use glue and glitter to decorate sheep
Watch Mrs. Feffenhoffer hurl glitter out window
Drink and bathroom break
Put on snowsuit and boots for recess
Emergency bathroom trip!
Take off snowsuit
Use bathroom
Put on snowsuit again
Recess
Take off snowsuit
Count five sheep
Tour schools looking for "fives"
Lunch
Practice writing the number five on whiteboard
Draw five sheep on whiteboard

Nap
Play at carpenter's bench
Try to fix broken sink in play kitchen
Talk with Mrs. Feffenhoffer and Sara about not telling Sara
she can't work with tools because she's a girl
Play at sand and water table
Listen to Mrs. Feffenhoffer's felt board story about the sheep
that was lost but then found
Pack up for home

That's what we did in kindergarten
All throughout the day
Learning here is so much fun . . .
I hope tomorrow's like today.

* * *

*It is so important to reflect on how it used to be. . . . Thank goodness
we've advanced beyond all of this. Right?*

Kindergarten 2.0

Follow responsibility list:
Hang up backpack
Put take-home folder on top shelf
Put on name badge
Take name card out of pocket chart and put in blue box
Put any mail on Mrs. Feffenhoffer's desk
Make lunch choice
Answer the Question of the Day by using the graph
Put stoplight on green
Shop for ten books
Look at books with book buddy
Have Circle Time/Morning Meeting
Check on stoplight—still green
Do alphabet aerobics
Check on stoplight—still green
Discover Letter of the Day—*K*
Listen to a story about the letter *K*
Check on stoplight—still green
Find something in the book that starts with the letter *K*
Circle *K* pictures on the smartboard
Create a four-page brochure on the letter *K*
Check on stoplight—still green
Draw *K* pictures on each page of brochure
Try to write *K* words under each *K* picture
Double-check that cover of brochure has a big *K* on it
If finished with brochure early, complete letter search page
hunting for large and small letter *K*'s amongst many other
letters that are *not* large and small letter *K*'s
Eat snack
Practice handwriting by writing the name of the Helper of the

Day using six different colors of crayons, which must be: red, blue, green, yellow, orange, and purple
Draw picture of Helper of the Day, focusing on details
Check on stoplight—still green
Listen to poem "I Like to Go to School"
Echo read poem "I Like to Go to School"
Choral read poem "I Like to Go to School"
Highlight every capital letter *I* in the poem "I Like to Go to School"
Put poem in poetry binder for future fun
Check on stoplight—still green
Read from independent reading book box
Lunch with recess
Check on stoplight—still green
Listen to Mrs. Feffenhoffer read aloud
Answer Mrs. Feffenhoffer's questions about the read-aloud
Study calendar
What day is it?
What month is it?
What is today's date?
Watch Mrs. Feffenhoffer add straw to pocket chart
How many days of school so far?
Watch Mrs. Feffenhoffer add penny to piggy bank
How much money is in the piggy bank?
What's the weather today?
What patterns can you find about the weather lately?
Go to music class
Take a drink on the way back
Stoplight moved to yellow for taking too long of a drink
Cut out math vocabulary cards
Check on stoplight—still yellow
Count to five
Count five spiders on the web

Count five apples on the tree
Count five coins in the lesson box
Count five fish in the sea
Count *more than five* wrinkles on Mrs. Feffenhoffer's face
Sit in the "thinking chair"
Check on stoplight—still yellow
Return to seat
Listen to book on "My Five Senses"
Learn "My Five Senses" song
Perform "My Five Senses" song
Kick Reginald during performance of "My Five Senses" song
Stoplight moved to red
Center time
Fill out behavior chart
Pack backpack for home

That's what we did in kindergarten
All throughout the day
We carved out time for everything
There's just no time to rest . . . or play.

* * *

My colleague Patti Rosenquist is an amazing kindergarten teacher, and she listens to and shares some of my concerns about the demands being forced on kindergartners these days. It's important, I believe, to assess how it really is. Our kindergarten teachers are under immense pressure these days, and what I have just described is a typical day in many kindergarten classrooms near the beginning of the year. Is anyone who is actually spending a day (or part of a day) in a kindergarten classroom happier now that we've upgraded kindergarten to the new 2.0 version? I was exhausted just thinking about this day—what if I (or you) were five years old and living through it?

Reading Orphans

Reading orphans.
We're out there, you know.
Moved too many times, developmental delays,
Or maybe something just didn't click fast enough for the
system.

It's amazing how we can be surrounded by other kids.
In a classroom year after year
And still feel alone, separate.

And the older we get, the greater the chasm.

We reading orphans look to you, our teachers,
Our one best hope for change.
You're frantic, frazzled, overworked, and underpaid,
We know.

But we look to you, still—

Using every attention-seeking behavior we possess
We're sending you a coded message . . .
Adopt Us.

· · · · · · · · ⊂∽∿∾⊃ · · · · · · · · · · · ·

*This poem was written on September 11, 2000, on a train bound for
Kirov, Russia. My wife and I were about to arrive at an orphanage to
pick up our wonderful son, Grayson, and bring him home. Our journey
made me think of the many students with reading difficulties who so
desperately need their teachers' help.*

First Grade

Squiggles.
Indecipherable, incomprehensible;
Foreign yet familiar.

Cherub faces eyeing pages
Filled to bursting with squiggles—
A banquet set for voracious appetites.

Prepare the meal with the utmost care,
Serve it on the fine china,
Don't forget the dessert.

Learning how to read shouldn't hurt.

· · · · · · · · · ══⟨∘∕∘∕∘⟩══ ·

Sometimes we forget what text looks like to brand new eyes that are trying to make sense out of it!

For the Phonics Advocate

First grade is where we learn to read!

I learned what a digraph is on Monday, and I haven't been the same since.

On Tuesday, I found thirty-two consonant blends and won a Tootsie Roll in class!

Did you know that sometimes the letter *C* is hard and other times it is soft? Now that I have completed seventeen workbook pages, I'm sure to remember.

Thursday was a tough day. We played *Who Wants to be a Reading Millionaire*, and I made it to $250,000.00! A question about *schwa* threw me, and I lost it all.

When Friday afternoon came, the teacher let us vote on what we'd like to do: have an extra recess period or read?

Everyone enjoyed the kickball game.

· · · · · · · · ══⟨ɷɷ⟩══ ·

I'll address the "Advocate" poems together because they really are a trio. The literacy "platforms" are really pretty funny when you think about it. If there were one best way, don't you think we would have found it by now?

For the Whole Language Advocate

This week was spider week in first grade!
Our teacher read us a Big Book about spiders.
We looked at spider pictures.
We made spider hats and wore them every day.
We pretended to *be* spiders, and I chased Susie under a table!
We sang songs about spiders.
We finger painted spiders.
We told our teacher spider stories, and she wrote them down.
This week our spelling words were all about spiders!
Our teacher says this is the way we learn to read.
Learning to read is fun!
I'm going to read a book on my own now.
"W-E-B? Does anyone know what this word is?"

Next week is ladybug week in first grade.
I can hardly wait!

For the Balanced Instruction Advocate

Scales, seesaws, and high-wire walkers—
A sense of balance makes them effective.

When you were told, "Throw out those basals, NOW!"
You heard, "You're narrow thinkers, and you've been doing it wrong all these years."

When you were told, "Write a scope and sequence for reading skills, NOW!"
You heard, "You've jumped onto a bandwagon, and you don't really know what you're doing."

Balance is a difficult state to achieve.
It takes dedication, perseverance, and equal support from all sides.

Teachers come equipped with those first two qualities.

Why doesn't everyone just stop bickering and help us out with that last part?

A Poem Written Exclusively for the Immense Pleasure of Those (Proud but Few) Who, 25 to 30 Years Ago, Had an SRA Kit in Their First-Grade Classrooms and Were Overachievers

Life's crowning moment:
Arrival at *aqua*.

. . . . ⸺⟨o/o/o⟩⸺ . . . .

I loved first grade. My teacher, Mrs. Porter, has always been a favorite—
she even came to my wedding! My fondest memory is of our SRA
Reading Lab and of being the first one in the class to make it all the way
to aqua, which was the final color. I've since befriended several other
"aquas."

Aliteracy Poem

Mrs. Thompson's second graders are amazing!
The principal says they can comprehend anything—
Even a medical textbook.

Mrs. Thompson's second graders are incredible!
The superintendent says their oral reading is completely
seamless—
Like the gentle flow of an eternal spring.

Mrs. Thompson's second graders are fantastic!
The P.T.A. president says they finished the reading workbook
and the phonics workbook in the first three quarters of the
school year!

Mrs. Thompson's second graders worry me.
You see, I'm the aide who works in the back of Mrs.
Thompson's classroom,
And I know something all those others don't.

Mrs. Thompson's second graders don't like to read.

* * *

The term aliteracy *is still new to many people. I hope that this poem will help introduce the term to more educators. Aliterate individuals are those who can read but choose not to do so. I often ask my graduate students, "If we teach the children how to read, but none of them want to, have we done our jobs?"*

A *Word* About *Vocabulary* Instruction

Teacher says we gots to work on improving our

Volacaberry?

Vobacalarry?

Vucbacaberry?

Words.

⸺

I recently read a very funny note from a parent who was trying to spell a word several different ways. She finally gave up and just wrote a simpler word.

Early Literacy Assessment

Quiz them—both orally and on paper
Listen to their retellings
Have them read from the basic sight word list
Select a variety of papers that demonstrate their progress in spelling
Administer and score an attitude survey for each one
Give them the unit pretests and prepare the end-of-level posttests
Prepare a cloze passage for them
See if each one can segment a word into phonemes
Take a running record on all of them
Review their standardized test scores
Make audiotapes of everyone's oral reading for the portfolios
Check with the reading specialist on the progress of caseload kids

Now let's see . . . seems like there was something else I was supposed to do by the end of the week. Hmmmm. What *was* that?

Oh. Goodness me, I nearly forgot.

Teach.

. . . . ━━◖◗◗◖━━ . . . .

Sometimes we get so busy preparing and administering assessments that we forget about the most important thing—teaching! This can also be true of those people removed from the classroom who are concerned with "monitoring student performance."

ABOUT GRAMMAR,
SPELLING,
HANDWRITING, AND
COMPOSITION

"I've Got a Semicolon, and I'm Not Afraid to Use It!"

My wife, my mother, and a handful of very close friends could all attest that I am rarely heard to utter the sentence, "I am impressed." It's not that I'm some kind of pessimist; quite the contrary, hope springs eternal with me. The world at large, however, dashes my hopes more often than I'd like to admit. I have all kinds of wild expectations that keep me from being impressed. I want politicians to tell the truth the first time, I want the drive-thru people to put the food I paid for in the bag they hand me, I want the person who said, "I'll call you back with that information this afternoon," to call me back with that information—before my death! I suppose, if I am honest, I think the bar is "set a little low" just about everywhere, making it terribly hard for me to feel impressed. And when I'm not impressed, I never pretend to be. It's a rule I adhere to without exception.

A good friend asked the other day, "What impresses you, Steven, really?" And without blinking I responded, "People who use semicolons correctly." I hadn't even realized that was going to come out of my mouth, but there it was. Sometimes it's great fun when you surprise yourself. Upon reflection, I'm not one bit sorry I said it. In fact, I will now add to that statement that if you know what a conjunctive adverb is and how to use it correctly (hint: a semicolon *is* involved), I might remove someone from my Five Favorite Friends list and use you as a replacement. Of course, at the crux of this entire matter is my deep concern that we may have an entire generation of young people who don't know how to write; in other words, (guess what grammatical construct I *just used back there?*) they don't have any decent command of written English. I realize that it is entirely unfair to lump an entire generation together; it could be that there are a great many who will go on to study English at Cambridge, but I seem to constantly run into the ones who can't tell a preposition from a pronoun, and whose idea of a big decision during the writing process is how to end a sentence.

I admit to being greatly concerned over low standards just about everywhere, but I am especially concerned about it in the field of education. What defies belief even further is the notion that no matter how gently we go about pointing out the writing deficiencies of others, we are in the wrong for having done so. Personally, I'm tired of hand-holding people who appear, on the outside at least, to be adults. Sometimes there is simply no nice way to say, "Your writing makes no sense and is fraught with so many mechanical errors I mistook it for the work of a second grader who's taking a wide range of medications each day at noon."

I'm going to be bold right now and put out there what I've been holding back for far too long. So here it is. I think teachers should be extremely competent writers. I think it should be expected of them, I think it should be demanded of them, and I think if they're not—and they know it—they should take whatever steps are necessary to fix it. I think the standards for kindergarten teachers' writing ability should be on par with those of high school English teachers. If you're a literacy coach, the bar is even higher. If you're a principal—look out—my expectation of you is off the charts. All kinds of unflattering commentary may now commence about me, but I don't care. I don't want to hear the excuses; I just want the bar raised without exception.

It's fair to say that our command of written English falls to some degree to the competence and dedication of our former teachers and professors; their instruction coupled with our work ethic (or lack thereof) is the basic equation that results in the way we write today. I'm curious, though, what happens when we discover that they failed us, or we failed us, or the combination of "us and them" produced a less-than-stellar writer—the writer we see when we look in the mirror. I can't tell you how many times I have had to share the unpleasant news with a preservice teacher that he or she has produced a text that has nearly led me to a quadruple bypass. I have then frequently been told, "I can't believe that. All my papers in high school said 'A. Nice job.'" Sadly, in some cases the students have brought in their high school papers—clearly marked just as they indicated—which means either that no one ever read them, or that no one who is a competent writer ever read them. And now, guess who's the bad guy for speaking the truth?

More disturbing yet, some of these folks don't *want* to hear the truth—and I'm not just talking about undergraduates anymore. I'm talking about anyone. I've tried to improve the writing of all kinds of teachers and administrators, restaurant managers, grocery store supervisors, various and sundry people at all levels of the airline industry—only to discover my popularity dwindling as soon as I broach the subject. No matter how delicately you try to sweeten up the news, you're a villain if you constructively criticize their writing, you're an old timer if you worry about their mechanics, and you're out of touch if you try to explain that a strong command of the written word can actually be influential and garner the respect of others. They're doing just fine buying used "kars" from the lot down the street with the misspelled sign, texting a friend that "I'll c u 2morrow" and assuming it's acceptable to write it that way as well, and providing all future written work in a simple sentence format to avoid detection by those of us who might notice errors that are certain to surface when their sentences advance beyond seven words.

And since I can't change the world, I am forced to take comfort in the little things. At least the semicolon key is still included on the newest version of the iPhone—for those of us who know how, when . . . and where to use it.

A Tale of Spelling Woe

Oh, hell—I can't spell!
I've tried for fifteen years.
And writing without spell-check
Brings a host of freakish fears.

Now I need to spell "kunnundrumn" (kunondrum?
konondrom? conondrom? cahnuhndrum?)
But I barely can begin.
With no history of success
It can be very hard to win.

My new teacher throws me *Webster's*
And I guess I shouldn't mind it.
But since I cannot spell the word—
I wonder how I'll find it?

· · · · · · · · · ══◦/◦/◦══ ·

And we wonder why some kids drop out of school?

Comma Man

One group of children who refuse to pay attention to usage rules for "the comma"
One disgruntled educator
No air-conditioning in Room 112
Two pieces of sandwich board, some old clothesline, and a purple Sharpie marker

Put them all together and what have you got?
COMMA MAN!

HE attacks direct addresses with all of his might
HE separates words in a series and puts an end to perplexing phrases
HE corners off appositives so they correctly rename their corresponding nouns

HE even joins compound sentences with the help of his sidekick, Conjunction Boy!

OOOOOOOHHHHHHHH!

NOW, they get it.

Who says we don't need June, July, and August off.

. . . . ⟨ɷ⟩ . . . .

I'm often accused, by those who know me well, of being willing to go to any lengths to make my point.

The Ivory Tower

Sometimes I get awfully tired
Of listening to *the word* coming down from the Ivory Tower.
Then, I remember—they're only trying to help,
And I rush to the defense when my colleagues attack.

And yet, on days when the *latest* word defies belief,
I, too, am tempted to become a deserter.

Grammar *minilessons*?
The word—no more than ten minutes if you're doing it
correctly.

A complete disaster in every classroom down our hallway.

But . . .

I have an idea.

There are exactly ten minutes
Between when music ends and physical education begins.
Could someone come down from the Ivory Tower
And teach plural possessives?

It seems that there would be just enough time.

· · · · · · · · ══⟨⟩⟨⟩⟨⟩══ ·

*Many teachers complain that university professors are too out of touch
with the classroom. I defend the "higher ed" crowd when possible, but
sometimes even I find the ideas being touted around the Ivory Tower a
bit impractical.*

Grrrrr! for Grammar

Grrrrr! for grammar
'Cause grammar is great!
Without it we'd face
An unthinkable fate.

Imagine, just try,
To conceive of a place
Where no one used grammar
Oh, what a disgrace!

Why, how could we read?
And how *would* we write?
I'd say correspondence
Would be quite a fright!

With run-ons and fragments
In all of our print,
And no punctuation to help
Not a hint!

Our verbs and our subjects
Would never agree.
Antecedents for pronouns—
We never would see.

We'd be fraught by misspellings,
So make no mistake.
A land without grammar?
Just too hard to take!

My good friend and colleague, Valerie Cawley, is the sharpest "grammarian" I've ever known. She has a wonderful command of the English language; moreover, she imparts to her students a desire to use language correctly. Under her tutelage, they begin to care—truly care— about the way in which they express themselves. This poem was written for her, in appreciation for all that she has done to inspire strong writers.

Spellingitis

I think I have a bellyache
Because I need a spelling break
I'm sick of learning all these rules
Invented by some language fools

There's not a one that's made to last
No, none of them are hard and fast
But still they drill us night and day
Then slyly say, "Oh, by the way,

This only works when *that* is true
And such and such *can* be a clue
But *only* when a vowel may
Be used in a *specific* way

And even then, you've *really* got
To check *one other* caveat!"

Well, I can solve this language mess—
Let's cancel all the spelling tests!

· · · · · · · · · ⟨ひ/ひ/ひ⟩ ·

The spelling rules of the English language are a constant source of
confusion. It's good to be reminded that not everyone is a "speller" and
to stay in touch with how the younger crowd might feel about all of these
rules and exceptions.

Milford's Mom

Whenever I call Milford's mom, the talking never ceases.
When Milford isn't doing well, she simply goes to pieces;
She wants him in at Harvard, and she wants him at the top,
You see, her endless prattling just never seems to stop.

On Monday she was crying, and on Tuesday she got sick,
'Cause Milford blew his "how to" speech and botched his
magic trick.
On Wednesday she got loony, and on Thursday, boy, she
screamed!
When Milford got a grade that she just *never* would have
dreamed.

By Friday she had had it, and she started acting rude;
She heard my voice come o'er the phone, and WHAM! She
came unglued.
She sobbed about his future, and she moaned about his
strife—
Then she blamed each living being he'd encountered
throughout life!

She exclaimed, "He'll never make it! I'm disturbed and so
distressed!"
Then I said, "I only called to talk about his spelling test."

* * * * * * * * * ＝◯◯◯＝ *

*This poem mirrors the experiences many teachers have when they make
a phone call to talk about a minor issue and get an earful of parental
woes and concerns over matters completely unrelated to the topic of the
phone call.*

Mrs. Peacock: Craftsman at Work

I have just created seventeen letter *p*'s
making absolutely certain that the *circle* part connects
with both the top line as well as that handy dotted center line
at precisely the points Mrs. Peacock suggested.

Prior to this amazing feat, I crafted,
with pinpoint precision, might I add,
fifteen heart-stopping letter *o*'s.

Each *o* was drawn to Mrs. Peacock's detailed specifications
including the small "curly-q" on top, which is not,
as Mrs. Peacock has pointed out on numerous occasions,
the hair on top of an empty smiley face.

Should my *p*'s pass inspection,
it has been suggested that tomorrow I shall graduate to *q*'s
which, Mrs. Peacock says, are the only truly elegant and
pristine letters in the entire English alphabet.

Who says second grade isn't chock full of pinnacle moments
and life-changing events?
Just ask Mrs. Peacock.

· · · · · · · · ═◦◦◦═ ·

Teachers at every grade level have yearly pet projects of which they are
immensely proud or certain skills or content into which they pour their
unbridled energies. Sometimes it's good to see ourselves through the kids'
eyes and have a laugh at our own expense.

Cursive Writing Sparks a Revolution

Attention everyone!

After spending the last thirty-three minutes
fussing over loops, curves, and slants,
I'd like us all to consider, once again, my earlier suggestion,
made even before all of this madness began.

Let's all agree to print for the rest of our lives and spend a lot
more time at recess!

Who's with me?!

⎯⎯⎯⎯⎯⎯⎯⎯⎯⎯⎯⎯⎯⎯⎯⎯⎯⎯⎯⎯⎯⎯⎯⎯⎯⎯⎯⎯⎯⎯⎯⎯⎯

*Why was cursive writing ever invented, and why do we want children
who can print decently to continue using cursive when they can't write
legibly in that form?*

Mail Drop

Teachers:

How would you like to receive over 100 letters
Every day
From people you didn't know
Who were only writing to you because
Someone told them that they had to?

Think about this
Carefully
The next time you start to assign your students
The task of writing

To
An
Author.

· · · · · · · · · · ═══◎/◎/◎═══ ·

*I promised myself, if I ever had the chance, I'd help all of the authors
who are begging teachers to stop assigning kids to write letters to authors.*

Staff Development

The district's in chaos!
Writing scores are drooping like soggy diapers.

They hired a consultant for us this fall,
Auntie Mame of the writing world, we called her.
She reviewed the students' writing from last year and told us,
"The children should *never* write to a prompt.
These children are stilted, formulaic writers who lack tone,
voice, and creativity.
That's the problem!

Just have them write about their *feelings*!
Let their unburdened, youthful ideas spill forth onto the pages
Like the rain showering down upon the parched Earth!"

The district then hired another consultant for us in the spring,
Writing Rambo, we called him.
After reviewing the students' writing from the fall, he told us,
"The kids should *always* be writing to a prompt.
These kids are wispy, superficial writers who lack logical
support, sufficient elaboration, and proper conventions.
That's the problem!

Just have them write to practice prompts, preferably three per
day!
Give them a clear, precise framework to latch onto and
Trust me, once they learn it, they will *never* let it go!"

The district administrators are now pressuring us to spend
our summer developing a brand new writing curriculum

based upon the recommendations of the consultants whom
they hired but never listened to.

They're paying us, of course.

We've decided to take the job and the money,
spend the summer vacationing with our families,
and turn in the old writing curriculum in brand new three-ring
binders.

. . . . ——⟨⟨⟨⟨—— . . . .

*I couldn't resist depicting an all-too-often-true scenario that occurs
in many school districts. I've heard countless versions of this type of
situation—except for the fictionalized ending, of course.*

Why the Teachers' Lounge Has a Door

A seasoned teacher nervously bites her lower lip
The day of reckoning has arrived

The State Writing Test Administration Manual grins
malevolently from the top of the stack

Pencils sharpened, test booklets distributed, directions
explained
Countless weeks of preparation are about to come to fruition

The principal enters and moves inconspicuously to the back of
the room, poised to observe

"Any last minute questions, boys and girls?"

A hand rockets skyward but forgoes acknowledgment,
"I thought you were going to *cancel* this writing test, Mrs.
Catalano?"
The principal's cocked eyebrow collides with the teacher from
across the room.
"Why, Cletus," she stammers. "That certainly is *not* the case!
Whatever gave you such a *silly* idea?"
A sly grin creeps onto the face of the precocious boy.

"I was walking by the teachers' lounge when you told Mrs.
Gulliford that you were worried the state writing tests were
going to turn us into a bunch of *mindless, mechanical* writing
robots!"

Many teachers are concerned that the pressure we all feel to turn out students who can write well—specifically for the state tests—may lead to overdoing the preparation.

A Poem About Kids Who Move into Your School District from a District Where They Do Too Much Training in Preparation for State Writing Examinations

"All right boys and girls,
Today, I'd like you to write a descriptive paragraph about
something you treasure."

"Mrs. Smith, may I please write this in a five-paragraph
format using both internal and external transitions in
combination with varying degrees of support and elaboration
so as to enhance the precision and specificity of my response
to the given writing prompt?"

"Matthew, dear, I just want you to write a simple descriptive
paragraph."

"But Mrs. Smith, I moved here from West Hampton Hills.
That's the only way I know how to do it."

· · · · · · · · ══════⟨⟩⟨⟩⟨⟩══════ ·

*This poem reflects a true story that happened to one of my wonderful
colleagues, Marilyn Jancewicz. We laughed for days over this one!
Nobody can tell it quite like Marilyn, but this is my best effort.*

Oops!

What do you *mean* those handouts you sent to my room five minutes before the bell rang and told me to stuff into the report card envelopes

(and that I randomly crammed into those envelopes in no systematized fashion)

were the students' *individual* reading and writing scores from the state assessment test?!

It's going to be a very long night.

"Hello, Mrs. McDetweiler, the *funniest* thing happened today! *Actually*, you'll probably find this quite amusing.
You see . . ."

· · · · · · · · · ══⟨ɷ⟩ɷ⟩══ ·

True story. Unfortunately, it's mine!

ABOUT JUNIOR HIGH
AND HIGH SCHOOL
LITERACY ISSUES

Mrs. Warner: A Radical in All the Right Ways

Mrs. Warner was, in the language of a bygone era (not one that I inhabited, mind you), "groovy." Though not a ubiquitous adjective of the early '80s, it was then and remains today the only descriptor in the lexicon that aptly describes the phenomenon that was my sophomore English teacher. She towered over us all, a slender but graceful giraffe in human form with large doe eyes. She was unlike any teacher I had ever encountered. In fact, I wondered on multiple occasions if her presence among us was a soon-to-be-discovered accident. Perhaps she had wandered out of some kind of "flower child" convention and into our local high school without any teaching credentials but decided she liked us and settled in for a short time? I'm not sure yet today that I'm entirely wrong about that because she wasn't with us long, and for that I have always been truly quite sad.

I learned a great deal from Charlotte Warner, and I'm sure I wasn't the only one. I became a writer, in large part, because I discovered that I *could* be—and it was in her classroom. I'm sure she would take no credit and would insist that, if in fact I possess any writing prowess at all, none of it is due to her—but she would be incorrect. I wrote more for Mrs. Warner and in her classroom than ever before. And the writing, as I remember it, didn't *feel* like a curriculum. Now, perhaps it was—students don't get down into the weeds on such issues—but I have a sneaking suspicion that the Mrs. Warner I knew could never have been stifled by a "here's-the-manual-and-a-matching-box" kind of curriculum that makes some teachers drools. I can envision her strategically losing such items for days on end and filling in the time with more authentic kinds of writing activities.

She was ahead of her time, I believe, by about twenty years. She published our work. Oh, it was nothing fancy—a dittoed packet with our pieces typed out. Typos abounded, but who cared? It was stapled with a cover note written about our best pieces, selected by her personally. What a vote of confidence! I didn't know about everyone else, but I wanted a piece in one of her packets every time she produced one. There was a sense of validation and pride that swelled within me each time I saw my work typed out in one of those packets that kept me awake at night; the entire process felt so authentic! I was a writer—Mrs. Warner clearly thought it to be true.

I vividly remember the day she glided about the room just after the bell, passing out a different 8.5-x-11-inch photograph to each of us. I looked at mine with complete disinterest. It was a dead field—not a wagon wheel, not a blue jay, not a cloud in the sky— just dead grass. I was less than excited and immediately noted that everyone else's photograph looked far more intriguing. Mrs. Warner then erupted with her typical exuberance, explaining that we should all take out "about twelve pieces of paper." A collective class gulp was nearly audible. I believe the great majority of us liked this woman, but she was clearly crossing a time-worn line in the sands of learning. Surely she had meant to say "a" piece of paper? Perhaps even "two" was allowable on a bright sunshiny day. Again I was forced to wonder about her teaching credentials. Any teacher I had ever met would have instinctively known that such a statement, made at the high school level, necessitated one or perhaps more bodyguards, yet she remained either unconcerned or oblivious—with her it was always hard to tell.

A few moments later she rocked my world by announcing that we should examine the photograph we had just been given and answer the question: "What is it about my photograph that is *fascinating?*" Reminder: I had been given a photograph of a dead field. She told us this was a very important question because, for the next fifty minutes, she expected us to tell the "story" behind our fascinating picture to the world through our writing. The thought struck me that twelve pieces of paper would not be necessary were a certain young man to craft the world's shortest story ever: *Everything died. The end.* I discarded the thought, though, as I knew it would never fly, and I did not want Mrs. Warner disappointed with me. Before the customary outcries of "How long does it have to be?" and "What if . . . ?" could even reach a respectable crescendo, Mrs. Warner repeated her charge: "Write the story that *is* the picture!" She announced she would answer no more questions and speak to us no further. "WRITE!" she proclaimed.

I looked despairingly at my dead field and put my head in my hands. What was I to do with this? A few minutes later, a California redwood was kneeling at my desk.

"Steven," she said, "I want you to tell a *great* story. This is your chance; don't waste it. Let the world hear your voice! I've always believed you had something to say. Now, come on. Let us hear what it is." I'm sure Mrs. Warner has long forgotten that moment. It would understandably blur into the conglomeration of the many moments throughout her career when she undoubtedly sensed a student feeling ill-equipped, and she moved to counter. I, on the other hand, can hear those words as if she spoke them to me only moments ago.

Mrs. Warner entered the piece of writing I produced that day into a leveled writing competition, and it won. It won! My teacher told me to write so the world could hear me, and when I did, she took the time to put it out there—into the world. My teacher believed in me, and she showed me that she did. What kind of a teacher does that? Perhaps the kind who somehow fights the system every now and then, or "loses" the system every now and then, whenever it interferes with "real" teaching. Every word I have written, of my own desire, since the day I won that writing competition has been *because of* Charlotte Warner, and perhaps *in spite of* what Charlotte

Warner was supposed to be doing on that day.

And despite the fact that I have never seen her again, I can assure you I have never, *ever* been without her when I am writing. It is her voice that shouts encouragement when I am discouraged, defends my honor when I am attacked, whispers hope when I am uncertain, and bolsters my confidence when I feel defeated. Most important, she is there, among the many teachers who are filling the balcony of my life, and she is always easy to spot in the crowd. Why? Because she celebrates every success with her own unique cheer—some unprecedented cross between a Comanche war cry and a general's call to arms. She's leaning over the railing creating a scene—arms flailing, feet stomping—I never know what it will be. But I always know it will be something that's *all* her. Mrs. Warner is not like any of the others; she never could be. And that, I feel sure, has made all the difference in more lives than just mine. I'll take the liberty of speaking for many of the other students who were blessed to call her their teacher when I say, "Wherever you are, Mrs. Warner, you can be sure that we wouldn't have it, or you, any other way."

The Book Report

The book report?
A last resort!
(That's always my informed retort)

Assigning one? An awful deed,
And so I have to intercede . . .

Before the kids all hate to read.

· · · · · · · · ══◄◖◗◖◗◖◗►══ ·

*I hate book reports, and I always have. I think there are far more
productive and motivating ways to engage kids with books rather
than assigning one of these horrific monstrosities. Conferencing about
books—teacher-student, student-student, student-parent—is a far more
personal and intimate way to learn what a student has captured from
reading text. Also, student-led book chats (when appropriate coaching
is provided)—where kids have an opportunity to encourage others to
read specific selections—provide a more authentic way for students to
demonstrate what they have read.*

The Transfer

Teaching in the junior high
—Oh what a thing to do!
To transfer up from second grade
They said, "What's wrong with you!

In junior high the kids don't care,
Just wait—some lazy lout,
Will tell you he won't read one book
Two months and you'll want out!"

"Those kids are *reading duds*," they say
"Their skills are just the pits,
And if they have to read in class—
You've never seen such fits!

In grade school's where you've got it made
Our kids still want to please,
And many of them love to read
And say that it's a breeze

But big kids *hate* to read and write
The testing shows they're low."
I face my colleagues and reply,
"That's *why* I want to go."

. . . . ⟶⟨∂/∂⟩⟶ . . . .

*I've taught at the elementary level and at the junior high level, and I
love them both for different reasons. Most educators I meet, however,
prefer one over the other. My heroine is Dr. Jill Cole, who moved
from first to eighth and second to seventh grade for many years with*

incredible grace and professionalism. What's more—she was fabulous in every grade level.

Why I Love Teaching Junior High

" . . . and so kids,
denotation is really just a fancy synonym for definition;
whereas, *connotation* refers more to the positive or negative
attributes that we associate with a word.

For example, there are many words that we look up in the
dictionary that have a *neutral* denotation
but, in fact, when we hear them,
they evoke strong negative feelings in us.

Can anyone think of word that has a neutral denotation
but a very negative connotation?"

I smile, preparing to bask in the glow of success as one of my
students makes the connection. "Yes, Arthur. Do you have an
example?"

"Oh, yeah, easy! *School!*"

* * *

*Some concepts are so difficult to teach, such as denotation versus
connotation. Although this particular incident is fictionalized, it is the
embodiment of my experience teaching junior high. When they finally
get it, they get you, too!*

Stage Fright

Knees knocking
Throat's dry
Speeches make me want to die!

Hands wringing
Voice shakes
Geez, oh boy, what *guts* it takes!

Eyes darting
Stomach churns
Three more weeks—then it's *my* turn!

* * *

This poem was written in honor of my colleague Kathy Bruni, who has trained students in the art of public speaking for many years. It's also written for all of those kids who are petrified to "stand and deliver" in front of a crowd. It's easy to forget just how far in advance their terror can truly begin.

Literature Circles

Circles of literature
Literature loops
Just pass out the books
And we'll get into groups

'Cause once my group's seated
We start to converse
And in no time we're quoting
Both chapter and verse

From a book we *enjoy*
And we *get it* no less!
We're in charge of our reading—
No need to get stressed

Let's keep the lit circles
And try them once more
These types of discussions
Are what reading's for!

. . . . ━━◦◦◦━━ . . . .

*My elementary and middle school students always loved the chance to
talk about books. Having "jobs" to do was a drag, they'd tell me, but
when we tried lit circles without any tasks the students generally came
back and asked for some "roles" and paperwork to help guide their
discussion. Perhaps they were a bit young, in some cases, to manage the
discussion with no framework at all. Still, when they wanted to try it
without the jobs and the paperwork, I always said, "Go for it!"*

Dissection

11:27 p.m.

I've just finished the seventh really terrific book that Mrs. Pennywise has assigned us for Academic English this year.

Too bad that, like all of the others, by the time her class ends at 10:04 tomorrow morning,

I'll hate it.

· · · · · · · · · ⟨∞⟩ ·

In writing the poems for this collection, I kept my ears open. Sorry to say that sometimes, this is what I heard from high school students. Does every book have to be evaluated to the point that there's nothing left to enjoy?

Censorship

Parents are enraged—
"What are they doing to our children by exposing them to that book?
Don't they care?"

Teachers are defensive—
"They have no idea how this book is being used or for what purposes!
Don't they trust us?"

Administrators are frustrated—
"This is a no-win scenario that's blown way out of proportion.
How can we satisfy everyone?"

Students are exempt—
"Everyone's talking about us, but no one asks *us* if we've been *damaged*.
Won't anyone listen?"

Parents want to protect their children.
Teachers want to educate their students.
Administrators want to provide a safe learning environment.

And the kids . . .

They just want to enjoy a good read.

· · · · · · · · ━━━━━⟨o/o/o⟩━━━━━ ·

Book censorship is a subject about which I am passionate. It is important to remember that, in most cases, would-be censors are acting out of a sincere desire to protect kids. Unfortunately, the media exploits the slightest hint of a question about a book to the point that entire communities are torn apart over issues that could be better handled outside the public forum.

So Honored

What do you *mean* my child can't be in honors?
Why everyone *knows* that if you aren't in *Honors* English
You spend the rest of your life flipping hamburgers!

What's wrong with you teachers?
Can't you see that he's gifted! Gifted! GIFTED!

Of course, you can't.
You can't see his giftedness because it's hidden behind . . .
behind
His *learning disabilities*!

Yes, indeedy-do, he has learning disabilities.
You never discovered them! We hid them from you!
We know what *you* people do to children with learning
disabilities.

No! None of that for *Terrence*. We hired Mrs. Farfanhoofer
for $200.00 a day to help little Terrence with all of his
homework for the last seven years. Ha! Ha! See, we fooled
you. You never found out!

Now then, you'll *have* to put him in Honors English
Or else you'll be guilty of discrimination!
We'll complain to the principal, we'll call the superintendent,
We'll petition the Board of Education!
We'll *force* you to put him in Honors English!

Lucky for Terrence he has parents like *us*.
Parents who know what's best for him.

Placement in honors-level classes can be a migraine-creating ordeal for teachers. Sadly, this poem is based on a real-life conference.

Lifesaver

Every day, Mrs. Warner has them take out their journals and write

And, at one time or another, most of them unknowingly allow their fragile emotions to melt into words in a safe, private place.

In the frantic, stress-filled, high school day
Mrs. Warner hopes she's found a way

To save some kids' lives.

· · · · · · · · · ⟨⟨⟨o/o/o⟩⟩⟩ ·

I had a high school English teacher, Mrs. Warner, who really sparked my desire to write. We didn't keep journals per se, but I know a lot of teachers today are asking high school kids to keep them. Our teens are under such pressure; journal writing is a good way to let them release what's churning around inside. It seems like the kind of thing Mrs. Warner would do, too.

A Cautionary Poem for Content Area Specialists

"I teach science—not reading.
If the kids can't read by the time they get to me,
It's because you *elementary* teachers are asleep at the wheel!"

[Pause.]

"Hey . . . hey, wait a minute . . . now wait just a . . . AHHH!"

Poor man.
Simultaneously peppered by one hundred sixty-three
sharpened pieces of anti-dust, high-velocity chalk.

He never had a chance.
God rest his soul.

. . . . ══════◦◦◦◦══════ . . . .

*The opening of this poem is based on an incident that occurred in a
school where I was doing some consulting work. By the end of the week,
the middle school science teacher had "seen the light" (he really is a
terrific guy), but I feared the elementary teachers were going to riot on
that first day!*

ABOUT READING ALOUD

The Statistical Significance
of the USPS

Christmas 2004 was a magical one for me. Our two oldest children were at the age where all things Santa are uber-mysterious and exciting, and the newest arrival in the Layne clan, Jackson Nathanael, was filling all of our days with energy and laughter. I look back, now, at a specific photo taken in front of the tree from that holiday, and I marvel: we had no idea what was coming.

Three days after that photograph was taken I was hooked up to a ventilator, paralyzed from the neck down, and fighting for my life. It wasn't an automobile collision or a freak accident. It was an autoimmune disorder called Guillain-Barre Syndrome. It struck in the middle of the night with a vengeance and, within hours, my life as I had known it was upside down. There were no warm assurances from any members of my team of sixteen doctors that I was going to ever have that life back. They would do their best—all anyone can do against one of the most mysterious autoimmune disorders that exists in the world today.

Though I have spoken publicly of those dark days on occasion, I have not written about them. I am still not, and may never be, ready to fully tell the story; in pieces, though, I am up to the task. And there is one piece that very much needs to be told.

It has been my blessing to teach with some truly extraordinary people. One of those, Lisa Owen, is nothing short of a teaching genius. I taught with her early in my career and, by the end of our first year together, we were finishing each other's teaching sentences. Though our paths eventually led in different directions, that kind of bond is never broken. I have no idea exactly how Lisa received the news of my critical condition, but I know it had to be devastating. Never one to sit idly by, she had to take action, and the action she took was inspirational to put it mildly.

My agent at the time, Anne Wilson, was handling queries from the literacy world at large, and my amazing wife was blogging for family and friends. Colleagues at Judson University were handling that part of my life, and all of those efforts amounted to a whole lot of mail arriving at the hospital every day. There came a point, though, when masses of letters began to arrive that very much belonged together. To make a very long story short, Lisa had crafted a letter and found a way to get that letter to a serious number of my former students. At its core, her letter basically said, "Your teacher needs you." And the letters poured in. I could not eat, I could not speak, I could not move, but I could listen— and every one of those letters was read aloud to me.

I'm sure I was inspired by those letters and heartened by them, but truth be told, I was on so many major drugs that I was frequently in and out of any true level of consciousness. I remember that the letters came, and that I was excited to hear my students' names, but I have very few tangibly vivid moments from those first several weeks that I can recall in great detail.

The letters were saved, as was every piece of mail that arrived during my many months of hospitalization. Two years ago, during the Christmas holidays, I opened the boxes of mail from 2004 and 2005 and began to relive it all. In short order, I felt inclined to organize letters from students into their own separate stack, and I read those first. I smiled and laughed through the first few, sharing in the fond remembrances of my former students, many of whom were now in college. I was beginning the sixth letter when I began to notice something in particular that the letters seemed to have in common. At first, I thought it was a trend or perhaps an unusual coincidence. I backed up and looked over the first few letters again—just to be sure I wasn't imagining it. No, there it was, consistently in every letter. I was so taken by this amazing situation that I left the letters on the table and phoned Lisa. I needed a copy of the letter she had sent my students, alerting them that I was gravely ill. Did she have it? Could she e-mail it? I was holding that letter in my hands a few minutes later, scanning it for some directive she must have given them that would explain the unusual and consistent feature I had noted in the first six letters. I came up empty. Lisa had urged them to write, with haste, but she provided no other instructions to them.

I returned to the mail pile, shaking my head in wonder, and continued through the stack. Those of you who love statistics would be overjoyed to hear that every single letter, without exception, contained the same unsolicited feature: they all mentioned titles of books I had read aloud in my classes. Even all these years later, my students were naming the books I had read to them. They still remembered. They had not forgotten. Some of them were going to be teachers and could not wait to share the same stories in their classrooms. Some wrote of their desire to read them to their own children. Some confessed to rereading them whenever they wanted to hear my voice and expressed how they never felt I was far away when one of those titles was near.

To those who might question the use of instructional time for reading aloud to students of any age, I would share this story. The data clearly demonstrate a level of statistical significance. Better yet, doesn't this story remind us of all the students who come to see us years later to share a fond remembrance of time spent with us? And what it is they often say? Oh, that's right! "Do you know what I remember *most* about you, teacher? It's workbook page sixty-seven!"

I hardly think so. It's more likely they'll be sharing the titles of stories that have seen them through the years. They'll be identifying books that have brought ongoing joy and that have provided comfort during times of deep sorrow. The message underneath it all will be that you have taught them how to be lifetime readers and cemented an understanding of the way a well-written piece of prose, poetry, or nonfiction text can stretch us, grow us, and change us.

If you're reading this book, there's a very high probability that some teacher did that for you. May I be so bold as to suggest that you grab an envelope and purchase a stamp? Sit down today, with a piece of paper and a pen, and write that teacher an old-fashioned letter. Then, send it off in the mail. You never know what a lifesaver that letter just might be.

Priorities

I must make time to read aloud
But there's so much to do
I heard Belinda (down the hall's)
On worksheet ninety-two!

And I'm on worksheet forty-three!
Our leaders can't find out
That I've been reading to the kids
My principal might doubt—

My calling, my commitment,
My devotion to the job
I'm married to curriculum
But still, I hate to rob . . .

The kids of time with books
'Cause when I bring a tale to life
Their wild excitement subs for
All their struggles and their strife

My kids know authors' names
And I read genres broad and deep
When they see me reaching for our book
I never hear a peep

They beg for one more page,
For one more minute, one half hour,
While my colleagues who won't read aloud
Are looking rather sour

I'll admit that I'm *old-fashioned*,
And I get some funny looks,
But my goal remains a classroom
Where the kids are hooked on books.

* * *

It is so easy to become convinced that there are more important things to do than read to the kids. I really doubt it.

What Is It That You Like to Do . . .

What is it that you like to do

With someone you care about

In a comfortable place

With a lot of expression

And with no interruptions?

READ ALOUD! (OF COURSE)

. . . . ⟨⟨⟨⟩⟩⟩ . . . .

This is just a fun "fooler" I've used to open several inservices on reading aloud to kids. I hide the answer at first. You wouldn't believe the answers people come up with! I thought it was so obvious what the answer should be.

Readin' Worries

I got some readin' worries and
They're buggin' me to beat the band
The stuff they're tellin' me in school
Is makin' me look like a fool!

Those digraphs are plumb hard to take
And *schwa* gives me a belly ache!
I'm sick to death of blends and such
And *no more vowels*—I've had too much!

The words I'm s'posed to know on sight
Are keepin' me up late at night!
And darn that word wall makes me frown
I'd like to say, "Let's tear it down!"

But teacher, she likes words a bunch
She reads to us right after lunch
And when she does I start to feel
That books just might have some appeal.

'Cause all us kids'll gather 'round
a-sittin', lyin' on the ground
As teacher reads aloud each day
My readin' worries melt away.

· · · · · · · · ━━⟨ɷ⟩━━ ·

*My students love it when I read to them in this voice. I use it for some
other poems that aren't in this book and for the voice of Harris when I
read aloud from Gary Paulsen's novel* Harris and Me.

Another Time, Another Place

Another time, another place,
Another life to live;
A different past, a valiant journey,
A friend with magic charms to give.

A promise spoken to myself,
An earnest, solemn vow;
Before the children leave my care,
They'll understand. Some way. Somehow.

That pages worn and tattered bear a tale that's fond and dear,
To someone out there, somewhere, it's a tale we need to hear.
And so I spend my moments on a search that knows no end,
Looking for the perfect tale to tell a child who's searching for
a friend.

Delight and wonder, terror, fear—both tragedy and care
When falling from the pages seem more possible to bear;
For sometimes, when I'm looking closely, hidden on a face,
I see a desperate need for me to take them
to another time, another place.

· · · · · · · · · ━━━<del>◦/◦/◦</del>╞━━ ·

Reading remains the great escape. I think we have more kids needing to escape today than we once did.

Observations From on High

I'd just begun Chapter 7 when Dr. Schleppenfeld,
Who has a bachelor's in education, a master's in English
literature, a doctorate in reading pedagogy, and a post-
doctoral degree in literacy research,

and

who serves as our district reading coordinator,
popped by my room for a visit.

He saw the eighth graders sprawled all over the rug,
breathless with anticipation while I paused to acknowledge
his entrance.

He looked the scene over curiously;
Appeared rather perplexed in fact.
Eventually, though, he wandered over to me, leaned down, and
whispered into my ear,

"Don't worry. We'll just forget this ever happened, and I'll
come back someday when you're actually teaching."

· · · · · · · · · ━━◦/◦/◦━━ ·

A scenario similar to this one was described to me by a good friend.
It's hard enough to find junior high teachers who will make the time
to read aloud to their kids, and then you have some bozo like this
who . . . never mind.

There's Something

There's something in their eyes

There's something in their hearts

There's something in their souls

That longs to hear a story

There's something in their eyes,
That sparkles like a gem;
Each time I tell them of a book I'd like to read to them.

There's something in their hearts,
A yearning deep within;
They're hoping I will take them to a place they've never been.

There's something in their souls,
Which craves the chance to meet;
The characters who seem to somehow make their lives
complete.

There's something in their eyes

There's something in their hearts

There's something in their souls

That longs to hear a story.

It's very hard to explain to someone who has never read aloud to a roomful of children how very captivating and exhilarating the experience can be. I feel it is my greatest privilege as a teacher—at every grade level.

Read to Them

Read to them
Before the time is gone and stillness fills the room again
Read to them

What if it were meant to be that *you* were the one, the only one
Who could unlock the doors and share the magic with them?
What if others have been daunted by scheduling demands,
District objectives, or one hundred other obstacles?

Read to them
Be confident Charlotte has been able to teach them about
friendship,
And Horton about self-worth;

Be sure the Skin Horse has been able to deliver his message.

Read to them
Let them meet Tigger, Homer Price, Aslan, and Corduroy;
Take them to Oz, Prydain, and Camazotz;

Show them a Truffula Tree.

Read to them
Laugh with them at Soup and Rob,
And cry with them when the Queen of Terabithia is forever
lost;

Allow the Meeker Family to turn loyalty, injustice, and war
Into something much more than a vocabulary lesson.

What if you *are* the one, the only one, with the chance to do it?
What if this is the critical year for even one child?

Read to them
Before the time, before the chance, is gone.

· · · · · · · · · ════⟋⟍⟋⟍⟋⟍════ ·

Of all the published writing that I have completed to date, this little poem has brought me the most attention. It is dear to my heart because it expresses so clearly my deep desire for people to understand the necessity of reading to children. There's so much the children miss out on if they are not read to throughout the grades!

ABOUT STANDARDS
AND TEACHERS

Have You Ever Been to Fullers Bookshop?

It had been a busy week for my friend Chris Topfer—functioning as hostess, escort, and driver as I provided author sessions in a variety of schools she serviced as literacy officer in and around Hobart, Tasmania, Australia. There had been several memorable moments throughout my time in Australia during what was my summer (but their winter) of 2011. In one of our first schools, I was speaking to the kindergarten students when one little girl scooted up against Chris—who was seated on the floor near her—and began to gently stroke Chris's leather boots as she listened to me. Chris, being a highly skilled and sensitive veteran primary teacher, allowed this young girl to lean in close and to semiconsciously move her fingers across the smooth, soft leather. This little one was clearly deriving a level of comfort and peace from physical proximity with a caring adult, and the image was a powerful one for me. As I addressed that group of youngsters, and witnessed this small girl, I was reminded of the comfort a teacher can bring. That ability to comfort and nurture students is surely one of the many facets of teaching that drew most of us to the profession.

As we drove on to the next school, Chris and I spoke of this little girl and of what was really going on with her. I was comforted as I considered what had just happened. There was sweet relish in knowing that in a world gone crazy with testing and accountability measures, standards, and new initiatives, we had bucked the system this morning. *Today*, for forty-five minutes, some boys and girls sat on a rug, listened to a published writer talk about where story ideas come from, laughed as he read a story aloud, smiled as they studied various illustrations that delighted them, and asked some of their most burning questions. And through it all, one little girl had a chance to cuddle up against a teacher and draw comfort from her. That's a vision of kindergarten that just makes my heart sing.

Swinging to the other end of the elementary spectrum—grade five—a girl from a different school posed a question later in the week that had my literacy world spinning backward on its axis. At the end of a particularly rousing session with these fifth graders, it was time for a Q&A about writing. With the littler ones, it can be quite a feat to actually elicit a question at all—let alone one that is on topic—but by fifth grade it is rarely a difficulty. As expected, various children were posing spot-on questions about writing books, my personal writing process, and various other details of authorship—the perfect end to a session! And then, I called on her—near the back row, pale faced but with a smile that radiated such energy you could not miss her hand hoisted high and waving frantically in my direction. "What's your question, darling?"

"Have you ever been to Fullers Bookshop?"

It was clear from her tone of voice that this location was only one slight step down in importance from Parliament House in her mind. I had indeed *heard* of Fullers, one of the lovely downtown bookshops, but I hadn't yet visited. "No, honey, I haven't been to Fullers Bookshop, but I have heard some wonderful things about it. Do you like to go there?"

I didn't think it was possible for this child to glow any brighter, but somehow she managed it. She gathered herself up on her knees to grow a bit taller and exploded with passion as she shared. "Well, yes I have. We went on excursion to Fullers Bookshop, and there were books everywhere for us to look at all we wanted. And I even had a vanilla milkshake."

One of the classroom teachers became misty-eyed; I caught that immediately and knew that there was more to the story of Fullers Bookshop than just what I was hearing. Later, as the children prepared to exit, that teacher took a moment to speak with Chris and me. She made sure that I understood that an "excursion" in Australian schools is what U.S. schools call a "field trip." She also explained that many of these children were from lower-income homes where books are a rare commodity. "We realized that many of our students had never visited a bookstore, and we felt it was vitally important that we, as teachers, make that happen for them," she told me. It was clear that it had paid off in spades.

Back in the hotel that evening, I was still ruminating over the question posed to me and the delighted child who set it out there. I was thankful for a group of teachers so in touch with the students that they didn't just take the same excursions that, perhaps, had always been taken in grade five. They were clearly thinking deeply about the needs of these kids. I wondered how many schools all over the world are carting kids off to the symphony, famous museums, or historical monuments because "that's what we always do" without slowing down to wonder if that's what they *need* the most.

That little girl is no longer in grade five, and I know that I am likely never to see her again, but her question has caused me to question the status quo in just about every way when it comes to literacy instruction. She also motivated me to take action when I returned to Tasmania in 2012 so that, if by some miracle I ever do meet her again, I'll be able to tell her that I have a new answer to her question, and my answer is this one:

"Yes. Indeed I have been to Fullers Bookshop, and thanks to you, my dear, I've discovered that the vanilla milkshakes there are *almost* as good as the books."

The Common Core

The Common Core has led to war
And some are walking out the door
They've had enough—it's really rough
And now they say they're getting tough

They aligned all of the standards
And they did that work themselves
Now the standards are in binders
On some long-forgotten shelves

Then they rallied to the clarion call
To leave no child behind
And they tested, tested, tested,
'Til the smartest ones resigned

Now the course of evolution
Has produce the Common Core
Some are jaded, some suspicious,
Have we walked this road before?

And I'm thinking (call me silly)
That reforms will always be
And I wonder, will we ever learn—
The teacher is the key!
What's really sad is when we're mad
We see the Core as only bad
But if we could look for the good
We all might win! I wish we would.

Those who have heard me speak on the issue are aware that I feel the CCSS have a particularly gaping hole in that literacy as an affective element is not addressed in any solid and consistent way. That being said, a lot of excellent work has been done on the CCSS that can be of significant benefit for the discriminating district, school, or teacher. I wish these large-scale ventures weren't so polarizing—when that happens, we all lose so much.

The Standards

Hooray for the standards
They keep us all in line
They've shaped up our curriculum
The district looks so *fine*!

The "Sup." is really perky
And the principal is swell
Even Imogene LaBamba,
School Board Pres., is looking well!

The parents are rejoicing
That their kids can read and write
And the teachers—they're just smiling
'Til the next set comes in sight.

························ ◦◦◦ ·····························

*Standards help those invested in education to identify the goals we
are collectively working toward. They are also a security blanket for
people who aren't working in the classroom. It's amusing that excellent
instruction doesn't necessarily change due to the release of standards; it
just gets typed under a new heading.*

Out-of-Date

A standard is defined as something agreed upon by general consent as a reliable basis for comparison.

The only problem that I have with *these* standards is that all of the people who generally consented to them are dead.

· · · · · · · · · ━━━━◁⊙⊘⊙▷━━━━ ·

While standards are a "buzz" topic right now, they won't be forever. When they aren't the hot topic, it's interesting to see just how l-o-n-g they're allowed to stay in place without ever being updated or reviewed!

Model Teacher

When he asks us to write,
Mr. Bensen writes, too
And if we read to him,
He says, "I'll read to you."

When the podium's open,
He shares willingly
What a model of teaching,
He's turned out to be.

I created this man. He's the teacher we're all striving to become. Some days we're closer than others.

Teachers

There she stands, a harbinger of hope in the hearts of her students,
An oracle;
Promising each trusting face that, *together*, they'll search for and discover the answers.
A resilient guide—around, under, over, and through
Every seemingly insurmountable hurdle.

There he stands, a developer of dreams in the minds of his charges,
A builder;
Laying the foundation on which tomorrow's achievements will be constructed.
A skillful muse—bringing untended notions out of the shadows
And into the light.

There they stand, architects of endurance in the souls of the children,
Believers;
Offering assurance that there's always an opportunity to improve and a chance to try again.

Passionate cheerleaders—shouting encouragement from balconies
Where they have reserved seats for a lifetime.

. . . . ══════⌒◦⌒◦⌒◦══════ . . . .

This is the toughest poem I've ever written. I've had a love-hate relationship with it for a solid year because it had to be perfect! After all, it was written for someone who does terribly important work, someone who is changing our nation every day, someone who is very special. This poem was written for you.

Sometimes Teachers Wonder . . .

Dear Mrs. Tuttingsgood,

Thanks for the extra time you spent with me on my spelling every Tuesday and Wednesday after school this year. The tootering really helped a lot.

Tommy

· · · · · · · · · ━◦◦◦━ · · · · · · · · · · · · · · · · · ·

This poem is based on a letter that my wife received many years ago. It had us laughing for hours. I still laugh out loud every time I think of it. Fortunately, she was his math tutor.

. . . and Sometimes We Don't

We read about beautiful, impressive farewells
    in movies,
        in books,
            on television,
                in the news.
When they say goodbye, there's always a happy ending.
And all is well.
But they can always tell what's going to happen.
    It's scripted.
        It's right in front of their noses.
           They don't have to worry.
              It doesn't matter.
This matters.

You've taught me so much, so many incredible things.
You've taught me the way to make my ideas fly
    My creations perfect
        My emotions detailed
           My thoughts soar
              And that deserves a thank you.

But how do you thank the person who changes your life?

I wish I knew.

But another thing that you taught me was to try. So here it goes.

Thank you Dr. Layne. Thank you so very much. Thank you for the way you've touched my soul, the way you've brought my writing to life. Thank you for the lessons you've taught me, the criticism you've given me, the memories you've created for me. Thank you for the opportunities you've offered me, the goals you've helped me achieve, the barriers you've helped me break, and the treasures you've helped me find.

And now advice.

Never stop. Never give up. Never hold back. And most importantly, never change.

You've found what every teacher strives for: the perfect way to teach.

Thank you for changing me.

You did.

(Written by Lauren E. Sprieser upon her graduation from eighth grade at Butler Jr. High School, Oak Brook, Illinois.)

This is the only poem in the collection that was not penned by me; rather, it was penned for me. My decision to include it was not based on a desire for self-gratification. I believe this poem is representative of a favorite note, card, letter, or perhaps poem that you have received . . . or one that is still to come! Such treasures remind us why we do what we do. I also wanted to give Lauren the exposure because I believe she will someday be a famous writer.